"It was a blessing to personal
and her beloved husband, Ba
apparent in Missy's latest boo.
explore their deepest emotions. Sharing her pain, grief, and vul
nerability will help those struggling with loss realize they are not
alone."
— Robin Roberts, co-anchor of *Good Morning America*

"Missy Buchanan's *Feeling Your Way Through Grief* is a masterpiece.
For those grieving the loss of a loved one, her reflections come
as a balm, like sharing a conversation with someone who really
understands. For everyone else, her words serve as a moving
reminder to treasure the small things in your relationships, and to
be grateful."
— Adam Hamilton, author of *Wrestling with Doubt: Finding Faith*

"This candid, powerful, and vulnerable series of reflections on her
own grieving process in the loss of her beloved husband, Barry,
is a powerful resource that helped guide my own emotional life
towards healing. If your heart is broken by the loss of someone
you love, give yourself a gift and take some time with this small,
simple, and anointed book."
— Michael Adam Beck, pastor, professor, author, and Director
of Fresh Expressions for The United Methodist Church

"Anyone who has lost a spouse knows that grieving is a lonely,
treacherous journey *through* excruciating pain which is never alle-
viated by easy answers or superficial assurances. In *Feeling Your
Way Through Grief*, Missy Buchanan becomes an empathetic, sensi-
tive, encouraging, and insightful companion on the journey. By
graciously inviting us into the intimacy and vulnerability of her
grieving, she provides a safe space in which to confront grief's
anguished struggles with emerging hope and the assurance that
we aren't alone."
— Bishop Kenneth L. Carder, Ruth W. and
A. Morris Williams Distinguished Professor Emeritus,
The Practice of Christian Ministry, Duke Divinity School

"Missy Buchanan names the countless moments and memories and questions that so many of us experience when we enter the community of the bereaved. She's offering the gift of companionship, of understanding, of solidarity – so much more solace than a book of "answers" or platitudes for those who are on the unbidden journey of loss. This book is indeed a companion as we grope in the darkness toward the promised light."
—Rev. Dr. Rebecca Bruff, author of
Trouble the Water and *Stars of Wonder*

"If you are experiencing the grief of the death of a loved one, especially a spouse, the gifted Missy Buchanan has written poignant, personal stories that make this the best book I know to help you in your painful time. I will be recommending this touching and practical book to the grieving people I counsel in my practice and to others I know who are grieving."
—Terry Parsons, Ph.D., D.Min., author of
Life-Changing Stories: Reflections of a Seasoned Therapist

"Welcoming us into her journey beyond the death of her beloved husband, Missy offers real-life scenes from daily experiences that open up windows into the Spirit that connects us all. While these stories may seem short and simple at first glance, they are written from a master's perspective on the journey from grief that takes us from feeling rootless toward a new and even-more-solid grasp of the Home that awaits us."
—David Crumm, founding editor of
ReadTheSpirit.com online magazine

Feeling Your Way Through Grief

Feeling Your Way Through Grief

A Companion for Life After Loss

MISSY BUCHANAN

UPPER
ROOM BOOKS®
NASHVILLE

Upper Room Books® website: upperroombooks.com

Upper Room®, Upper Room Books®, and design logos are trademarks owned by The Upper Room®, Nashville, Tennessee. All rights reserved.

ISBN: 978-0-8358-2065-3
Epub ISBN: 978-0-8358-2066-0

Cover design: Emma Elzinga, Inksplatter Design
Cover imagery: Illustration edited by Emma Elzinga, source Freepik.com
Interior design and typesetting: PerfecType | Nashville, TN

Printed in the United States of America

This book is dedicated
to my beloved husband, Barry.

Love you times eternity times infinity times forever.

Contents

Part II—Everyday Grief

Part III—Grief Through the Year

Introduction

No one wants to go on the journey through grief.

My husband, Barry, was both my rock and my soft pillow in this earthly life. When he died, I was devastated. I immediately went to my personal library to search for books on grief. Since I am a writer and speaker on topics of faithful aging, I already had many resources on my bookshelf. My church, the funeral home, and dear friends gave me other books on grief. During the early months following Barry's death, I discovered that most of these books failed to hold my interest. No doubt they were well written and offered helpful information for understanding grief, but at the time, they felt too lengthy and laborious for my scattered, fragile mind. I yearned for simple words that spoke directly to my broken heart.

So, I pivoted to my own way of processing grief. I began to write snippets from my life in the aftermath of Barry's death as if I were speaking directly to him. Writing became an outlet for the tsunami of deep emotions I was experiencing as I navigated this difficult season. With no filters or expectations, I just wrote what my heart was feeling in real time.

The result is this book, which offers no prescriptions or steps to follow. There are no Bible verses to memorize or homework assignments to be completed. It is all about exploring emotions as a way forward. It is your invitation to grope alongside me in this darkness of grief.

The first part provides snapshots: small, intimate moments that caused grief to bubble up unexpectedly. The second part shares experiences of ordinary grief, those moments we encountered before our loved one passed and now come to with a completely different mindset. The last section includes seasonal or holiday reflections from the first year after my husband's death. These sections are intended only to provide organization to the meditations included: They in no way are intended to instruct or direct your grief.

My prayer is that by sharing my own pain and vulnerability, you, the reader, will take comfort in knowing that you are not alone. Though your experiences will differ from mine, you may discover that we share many inner thoughts and feelings. Most of all, I hope this book will be a safe place for you to explore your deepest emotions as you move forward on this unwanted journey through grief.

Part I

Snapshots of Grief

Rocking Chairs

The pair of rocking chairs on the front porch are empty now, except for the colorful pillows propped against the chair backs. They are silent and still, moving only if a storm blows through, causing them to do a wobbly dance. The thought of going to the porch to sit in my rocking chair without you is just more than I can bear right now. I have so many tender memories of late afternoon conversations on that porch. We sipped cool beverages under the whirring fan. We waved at neighbors walking their dogs in the park across the street.

During the pandemic, the porch was our refuge, a safe place to venture out into the world while the virus raged around us. We rocked and dreamed of vacation destinations. We FaceTimed with the grandkids. We talked about world problems and what to have for dinner.

Now I wonder if it will ever feel right to sit in my rocking chair again, knowing that yours is stilled by death.

———◊———

What is something that once brought you peace but now makes you uncomfortable?

Door Handle

Today the handle of the back door fell off into my hand as I went to the backyard to water the flowers. I stood there holding it, wondering what to do. It was the same door handle that came loose last summer as you were going outside to grill chicken-sausage kabobs for our lunch. I didn't pay close attention to how you fixed it, but you had it back on in just a few minutes.

This time, I manipulated the handle in every way I could, trying to get it to slide back on. I even watched a video on my smartphone to see if I could make sense of it, to no avail. The door handle is still off, with only the deadbolt in place to hold the door closed until I figure out what to do next.

Determining the next step seems to be my mantra these days. What do I do now? How do I proceed? Who do I call? Life seemed easier when there were two of us to decide the next step.

———◊———

Reflect on a recent time that you had to figure out the next step without the support of your loved one who has died.

Pumping Gas

Today I pulled up to the gas pump, put my head on the steering wheel, and wept.

I am fully capable of putting gas in my car. I have done it for years when I have been driving alone and needed to fill up. But if you and I were together on a road trip or running errands around town, you always hopped out of the car to pump the gas, even if you were in the passenger seat. It was just another one of those little things you did for me as a kind gesture, a small act of love. You'd gather empty cups or trash from the console; you'd clean the bugs off the windshield; you'd check the air in the tires.

I miss all the little ways you made me feel special . . . and safe.

———◊———

What small gestures did your loved one do for you that made you feel special or safe?

Greeting Cards

Today I rummaged through your drawer and discovered a stack of greeting cards I had given you over the years. Some were in celebration of anniversaries and birthdays; others were for Valentine's Day and just because. As I plopped down on the sofa to re-read each card, my heart was tendered by the idea that you had not tossed them in the trash after a few days. You must have considered them more than an obligation for a special occasion. Unbeknownst to me, you had saved them at the bottom of your sock drawer.

Sorting through card after card, I realized that each one had a familiar phrase written in my own handwriting. It was something I had coined years ago and penned on every card before adding my initial. *Love you times eternity times infinity times forever.* Sometimes I substituted the multiplication sign for the word *times*, but the message remained. It was my own way of recognizing that the word *love* by itself didn't seem to carry the weightiness of my deep feelings for and commitment

24

to you. I wanted it to convey more. Looking back, I suppose it was a silly practice, but I meant it then, and I still do.

———◊———

What is a habit you created to express your deeply-held feelings for your loved one through the years?

Tapping on the Window

In our empty-nest years, we loved road trips and navigating new places together. You liked to poke fun at me for the way I tapped on the window whenever I saw an interesting sight that I didn't want you to miss. I'd peck on the glass and say, "Look at that old house with the wraparound porch!" Or "Don't you think those wind turbines look like ballerinas?"

If you were reading a book or playing a game on your smartphone in the passenger seat, you would stop and look up. If we had questions about a specific sight, you'd Google it and read the information out loud.

I don't tap on the window anymore. There is no one in the car to share the scenic vistas or the quirky sights that pass by the window. And it feels so lonely.

———◊———

What is something you once shared with your loved one that now makes you feel lonely in this season of grief?

Sprinkler System

I had a startling thought as I opened the drapes this morning and looked out across the grass that is turning from winter brown to green—the sprinkler system! Summer is on its way, and I have no clue about the zones for the sprinkler system or how to set the automatic timer. It's just another one of those day-to-day tasks you fulfilled without fanfare. Sure, I watched you fiddle with it from time to time, but I didn't really pay attention except to alert you when I noticed a broken sprinkler head making water shoot up like a geyser.

The thought of having to learn another new thing in this season of loss drags down my spirit like an anchor drudging the muddy bottom of the lake. I'm so tired of having to learn things that you did so effortlessly. I am confident I can learn to do most tasks eventually, but I'm finding it hard to muster up the enthusiasm.

———◊———

What is something that you have had to learn to do since
your loved one died that you didn't really want to learn?

Coffee Mug

The mornings are just not the same. Though I still get up when it is dark outside, there's no one but me to push the button on the coffee maker now. Almost always, you set up the coffee maker the night before then brought me the first freshly brewed cup in the early hours. Now, except for the occasional gurgle of the coffee maker, silence fills the morning. There is no tinkling sound of your spoon hitting against the mug as you stir a bit of sugar into your coffee. There is no one who smiles at me and says, "How was your night? What's on your calendar for today?"

This morning, I opened the cabinet to retrieve a cup, and the tears began to roll down my cheeks. The sight of that silly coffee mug featuring your favorite TV show left me undone. For years, I had threatened to toss that faded and chipped mug into the trash. But now I'm glad I didn't.

———◊———

What is your favorite memory about
mornings with your loved one?

Shoes

The night you died, you left your shoes under the coffee table next to the sofa. They were resting in the same place where you often slipped them off as we curled up to watch an after-dinner documentary or light-hearted movie. For a few days after you died, I intentionally left the shoes under the table because it was a strangely reassuring image. They seemed to say that soon you would peer around the corner with a sheepish grin on your face, asking, "Have you seen my shoes?"

On your side of the closet, I find your beach sandals, a pair of never-worn house shoes, walking shoes, and two pairs of dress shoes. There's also the wooden shoe-shine box from your college years beside a chair where you would sit to shine your shoes on Sunday mornings. When I went out to the garage this morning, I passed by your old, worn-out tennis shoes, designated for yard work. They are still caked with mud from a time not long ago when you ventured into a rain-soaked yard to clip fresh greenery for my table arrangement.

I felt a sudden urge to slip off my flip-flop and step into your old tennis shoe, as if it might somehow bring you close. Immediately, I felt a rock in the bottom of your shoe. I recognized it as another reminder of the persistent agitation of grief. Even as I strive to move forward, I am learning to walk with the rock of grief in my shoe.

———◊———

What compels you to move forward despite constant reminders of grief?

Water Feature

When we downsized and built our smaller home, you worked with a landscape designer to create a unique water feature for our small backyard. It was your passion project to re-create a scene from nature: a three-foot high waterfall that tumbled over large rocks, couched with lush trees, bushes, and flowering plants. Whenever the weather cooperated, we enjoyed eating lunch together on the patio, listening to the soothing sounds of the splashing water.

It always warmed my heart to know how much you loved that water feature. Then just days before you died, the water feature mysteriously stopped working. You called the repairman, who promptly put us on a waiting list for repair work. In the meantime, the water feature remained still and quiet. The rocks were dry and lifeless without the cool water spilling over them. Then you died, and my world went mute.

Today, I will just sit in this grief and look out at the water feature. The water feature has been repaired:

the water flows over the rocks once again. It has been
repaired, though my heart has not.

——◊——

*What sounds remind you of your loved one who
has died? In what ways have you experienced
dry, lifeless living on the journey of grief?*

Tell Me a Story

You always knew that I'm a storyteller at heart. I love stories, and I loved to hear your stories even when you thought they were not important enough to tell. If I was having trouble going to sleep, I'd turn to you and say in a childlike voice: "Tell me a story." Unless you were already softly snoring, you would respond, "A story about what?" Then I would give you a litany of possibilities. "Tell me about a summer day when you were a kid. Or tell me about your grandfather who lived in Colorado. What was your favorite class in high school?" I loved hearing your tales of growing up in small-town America with tree-lined streets and a commanding courthouse in the middle of the town square. Even if I had heard the story previously, I welcomed hearing it again.

When we ate at our favorite pizza place, we'd take turns asking each other questions printed on a stack of cards that the restaurant kept at each table. You told stories about serving in the military and about your first job post-college. I shared tales of road trips and church camp from my childhood. Looking back, I regret that there were stories I never got to hear. I needed more time to ask for more stories.

———◊———

What story do you wish your loved one
could share with you now?

Words

There are times when I'm getting ready for bed that I realize I have not uttered a single word out loud that day. Not one word. Gratefully, those days are rare, but they occasionally do happen. Even those days are filled with texts, emails, and social media comments, but sometimes, there are no audible words. No real conversation between two people.

To be honest, those silent days feel easier in some ways because I don't have to be concerned that my voice will crack when trying to respond to the question about how I'm doing. Just hearing those words sometimes causes me to choke back the tears until I can say, "I'm okay until I'm not," a phrase I've borrowed from my recently widowed brother.

Don't misunderstand. Our kids are wonderfully attentive, but timing phone calls is tricky for all of us since they are scattered around the globe. And to be honest, there are days I don't even feel like talking on the phone or meeting up with friends. I miss those easy conversations with you throughout the day. I am learning that silence is sometimes a great burden to bear.

———◊———

Have you experienced days without having an audible conversation? How does that make you feel?

Signing by Rote

A church friend fell and broke her hip. As soon as I received word of her surgery, I went to my stash of cards and pulled out a *Thinking of You* card to put in the mail. I quickly signed our names.

Both of our names.

It's such a natural thing to do, writing your name next to mine. I've done it for so long now. It is an ingrained habit. It is almost as though I could write our names together in one swoop without even lifting my pen between the words.

I had to throw the card away and get another to write my name without yours. How long will it take before I remember that it's just me now?

————◊————

What is something that suddenly jolted you into remembering that your loved one has died?

Soap

Maybe it is a little bizarre that a bar of soap makes me think of you. Not just any soap, but your favorite brand of soap that left you well-scrubbed and smelling clean and fresh. You always preferred bar soap over body wash for your early-morning shower. If I were in the kitchen preparing breakfast while you showered and dressed for the day, you'd sneak up behind me and give me a surprise hug. So many mornings, I would get a whiff of your freshly washed smell that was far better than the most expensive cologne.

Now there are more than a dozen bars of soap stored in the bathroom cabinet, since I bought them in bulk not long before you died. I will use them, one by one, but the scent will never be as lovely as it was on you.

———◊———

What smell reminds you of your loved one who has died?

Outdoor Grill

The outdoor grill is still covered in a thick layer of dust, the result of a construction crew preparing to build a new house on a nearby lot in our neighborhood months ago. For many days, the dust swirled around us and left a grimy film on the windows, outdoor furniture, and your grill. You said there was no need to clean it until the bulldozers had finished their work.

After you died, I had the windows cleaned, and I washed the table and chairs. I don't know why, but I didn't bother with cleaning the grill. Now the powdery coating is a stark reminder of how much life has changed.

You are not here to grill steaks and veggies. You are not here to cook hamburgers for friends or family. The truth is, I have absolutely no interest in grilling for myself. I am not even sure I know how to safely turn on the grill. Maybe that will change. I don't know how long it will be before I wash the dust away, or if I ever will.

————◊————

What's something that you have no interest in doing since your loved one died? Why?

Books

I've been giving your books away one by one. On many Sunday mornings, I tote a few more volumes to the little library created in the corner of our Sunday school room so interested class members can read them at their leisure. Many are titles about US history, biographies, or memoirs. Others are books on spiritual formation or leadership.

As I sort through more titles, I realize that I should have told you how much I admired the way you tended your mind as you grew older. I was inspired by your intentional effort to continue to learn and grow. I noticed when you pushed back in your chair and immersed yourself in a lengthy book about US presidential history. It's no wonder that when we visited presidential libraries or historic sites during our travels, your eyes lit up as you shared tidbits of information from your readings.

I remember the time we visited our daughter in New York City not long after you had completed a thick book on the building of the Brooklyn Bridge. As the three of us walked the length of the bridge together, you told us stories about its construction and the mishaps and challenges the builders faced. It's a tender memory tucked away in my mind. Now as I reflect on those books, I realize how you inspired me to grow and learn too.

———◊———

*In what ways did your loved one inspire you
to be the best version of yourself?*

Shrimp

Today I am sitting in a local chain restaurant at the airport waiting for my flight. I have ordered a shrimp cocktail and salad, just as we always did when we flew out of this terminal. When the chilled shrimp arrives on a bed of ice, I grab one, holding the tail like a handle, and dip it into the red cocktail sauce.

With the first savory bite, I have second thoughts. Maybe I should have ordered something else this time. We always shared the shrimp cocktail—five for you, five for me. Ten large shrimp is a lot for one person. What was I thinking? Suddenly I feel a pang of sensory overload: the chilled shrimp, the scent of horseradish in the cocktail sauce, the lovely presentation on crushed ice.

The scene brings back the memory of a game we played when eating shrimp. You would eat a shrimp, then hold up the skeleton like a trophy, proving that you had cleaned every bit of meat from the tail. In this moment, I can visualize you sitting across from me with a cute smirk on your face. Now I'm sitting at the restaurant table by myself, staring at the remains of shrimp through watery eyes. The aftershocks of death can be so unexpected.

———◊———

How has food triggered an emotional response
for you during this season of grief?

Wallet

Your wallet is in the top right-hand drawer of your desk, in the same place where I put it just days after you died. The kids and I opened it briefly to secure your credit cards and such, then closed it again and placed it next to the box of unused checks from the bank, as if putting it away would somehow lock away the pain. I just wasn't ready to deal with it then, but now the time has come.

I tenderly lift your timeworn wallet to my face to smell the old leather. The wallet still has its slightly curved shape because of the years you carried it in your back pocket. I crack it open and see your face looking at me from your recently renewed driver's license. In all the slots there are reward cards, business cards, insurance cards, pharmacy cards, and an unused gift card from a local restaurant along with a receipt from your favorite barbeque place. There are two voter registration cards, one current, one expired. In another slot, there are two neatly folded papers. One is your real estate license and the other is your decades-old discharge document from the US Air Force. I smile to myself as I think about why you bothered to carry your military discharge paper in your wallet. Perhaps it was your proof to get a complimentary Veterans' Day lunch at an area cafe.

In one last slot, there is a photo of our children that is wrinkled and yellowed with time. I do a quick mental calculation and realize it is almost forty years old. The floodgates open; I cannot hold back the tears. Sorting through the contents of your wallet feels like another one of those intimate tasks brought on by death. I look at the remnants of a life well-lived scattered across the table. It makes me sad to think we will never be able to use the restaurant gift card together.

———◊———

What is a task you have put off because you weren't prepared to face it? What helped you to get ready for it?

Awkward Meeting

I ran into an acquaintance of yours today. It was someone I don't know well, but I remembered seeing him
at your funeral. I had not seen him since that day at
the church, and it seemed he wished to be invisible
as we made brief eye contact in the store aisle. I felt
sorry for him because he was obviously uncomfortable
being around me. I spoke first, then he made a clumsy
attempt at a response. Maybe he was trying to decide
if he should mention your name or ask me how I was
doing. He did neither. He just said something about
it being a beautiful day and moved past me as quickly
as he could. Even in the brief encounter, his avoidance
was obvious. I felt as if I were wearing a scarlet let-
ter *W*, an insignia that signaled I'm the new widow in
town.

------◊------

Have you experienced others trying to
avoid you in this season of grief?

Cardinal

Just days after you died, a friend drove to our house for a visit. She sat in her car for a while before coming to the door because she didn't want to frighten away a bright red cardinal that was sitting on our mailbox. I have often heard people talk about a cardinal being a messenger from heaven following the death of a loved one.

I really don't know if God has anything to do with sending a cardinal to bring comfort, but I do know there's a cardinal that loves to splash in our backyard water feature. I look out the window and get a glimpse of him flying from a nearby tree before landing on a big rock where he flits about in the falling water. It makes me smile. For now, that's enough.

————◊————

What is something in nature that has brought a smile to your face even in the loneliness of grief?

Teamwork and Balance

Today I am staying by myself at a lovely hotel in another city. For the first time since you died, I had to figure out the mechanics of an elaborate shower system without your help. You were not there to tinker with or explain the how-tos of this complicated shower-spa. When I finally managed to get an acceptable temperature and water stream, I turned too quickly and momentarily lost my balance. It made me think—what would have happened if I had fallen in the shower? Who would have known?

These days, I feel like I'm trying to ride a bicycle-built-for-two by myself. We were more than husband and wife. We were a couple, but we were also a team. Now it's just me trying to balance and peddle the tandem bike by myself. It's awkward and it's hard. For all these years, we have been there for each other as caregivers and encouragers. If one of us had the flu or was recovering from surgery, the other was there to bring soup and medications. You pushed my wheelchair when I fractured my heel. I helped you dress and put on your shoes after your shoulder surgery. You took on every home repair task, and I created your real estate newsletter. We constantly leaned on each other's abilities and strengths. We balanced each other and shared the effort. Now I must try to ride the tandem bicycle alone.

————◊————

How have you struggled with balance in your life now that your loved one is not there to share the effort?

Shattered Glass

Today I dropped a glass on the kitchen floor. It shattered into countless tiny shards that skittered across the tile. I stood there in my pajamas, barefoot, staring at the mess I'd made. In the past, you would have come running from another room at the crashing sound. You would have consoled me and reminded me to put on my shoes. Before I could have asked for help, you would have grabbed a broom, and I would have retrieved the dustpan. Together, we would have swept up the sharp pieces of broken glass. On the day you died, my life shattered into countless shards, but now you are not here to help me sweep up the brokenness.

———◊———

In what ways have you felt shattered by the loss of your loved one? How can you hold space for a comforting memory even in the uncertainty of grief?

Puzzle

Today I worked on a 100-piece puzzle with our youngest grandson. We propped up the lid to the box so we could see the picture we were trying to recreate. We joined the pieces one by one to create the outline of the puzzle, then we began to fill in the rest of the picture. As we sorted out pieces by color and shape, we talked about you. I want to encourage him to talk about his Poppi. I want him to remember the fun times he had with you, playing table games and riding a gondola up the mountain.

While we talked, he carefully fingered each puzzle piece before trying to fit it into place. It wasn't long before we had only a dozen or so pieces left to finish the puzzle, so I leaned back to let him complete it on his own. Soon he announced, "There's a missing piece!" He got on his hands and knees and scoured the rug beneath the table, but the puzzle remained incomplete.

That's how it feels now that you are gone. The picture is incomplete. Unfinished. Though the other ninety-nine pieces are in their rightful places, my eyes go to the space where the missing puzzle piece should go. My heart does too.

———◊———

How do you experience the missing presence of your loved one in ways that others might not understand?

Tears

Since you died, there has not been a day when I haven't cried at least once. Not a single day. No matter how busy I am, something will happen to cause warm tears to slide down my face. Sometimes it's a conversation with a friend. Other times, it's a photograph of a smiling you that pops up in the digital frame that I pass in the hallway. Sometimes it's opening the mailbox to discover a piece of mail addressed to you or searching through your desk for a paper clip. One thing I'm learning on this journey through grief is not to be afraid of tears. I believe they will come as long as they need to flow. There is no shame in tears. Only love.

———◊———

How accepting are you of your own tears while you grieve? Do you try to hold them back? When? Why?

Sea Glass Necklace

A day or two after you died, my thoughts pivoted from planning your celebration-of-life service to what I should wear. Though I was mourning deeply, wearing all-black just didn't seem like something you would have wanted. I began to sort through my clothes, trying to find the right outfit for the occasion. Not too drab, not too bold.

I pushed hangers back and forth trying to determine the appropriate look for a service that was to celebrate the love of my life. Should I wear dress pants and a flowing top? A skirt? A dress? Looking for inspiration, I opened a drawer and saw my drawstring travel jewelry bag. I had not unpacked the jewelry since we had returned from Cabo just a few weeks earlier. Inside was the turquoise sea glass necklace you had bought me years ago as we walked through a quaint Florida beach town. Uncharacteristically, you had suddenly stopped at a store window, staring at the long sea glass necklace hanging on a large piece of driftwood. You said, "That necklace looks like you. I'd love to buy it for you if you like it too." While I ducked into a nearby ice cream shop to get us single dips, you went inside the store and bought the necklace.

On the morning of your service, I put on a turquoise pantsuit and wrapped the long sea glass necklace around my neck. The turquoise color reminded me of the Caribbean waters we enjoyed so much on trips to St. John. Satisfied with my choice, I glanced into the mirror, then gave thanks for waterproof mascara.

———◊———

How did you decide what to wear at your loved one's funeral? Do you have a piece of jewelry or clothing that makes you feel especially close to your loved one?

Food

These days I'm not in the mood to cook. A carton of eggs or a gallon of ice cream often lasts longer than its expiration date. Now that you are gone, the joy of cooking has dissipated.

Even before you died, I was cooking far less than when we were raising our family. In our empty-nest years, we had grown accustomed to dining out at our favorite local restaurants several times a week. In fact, the waitstaff knew us by name and could predict our orders before we even sat down: salmon and spinach salad at one, brisket tacos and *elotes* at another. Before the pandemic, we would team up for a grocery store run. We used the divide-and-conquer method, splitting up our list according to the aisles and then meeting in the middle before checking out. During the pandemic, we learned to rely on grocery delivery or online pickup.

Nowadays, I rarely enter a grocery store, much less with a list and a plan. Instead, I've become accustomed to ordering groceries online and making simple things like turkey-and-Swiss-cheese sandwiches with apple slices on the side. Maybe one day I will elevate my culinary habits. For now, though, I'm satisfied keeping one eye on nutrition and another on simplicity.

———◊———

*How have you changed your cooking and
eating habits during this time of grief?*

Part II
Everyday Grief

Praying in Church

Like people routinely do, we sat in the same pew almost every Sunday morning. We even laughed about being able to identify our row without counting the pews because there was a tiny sliver of paper stuck between the cushion and the pew back that had somehow evaded the housekeeping staff for years. You always reached out and held my hand at the beginning of every prayer. It was a way we shared our faith, quietly . . . privately.

Now that you are gone, I have moved to another pew so I can sit between dear friends who understand when my eyes suddenly flood with tears. Now I bow my head and fold my hands in my lap. I take comfort in my church family who love me well in your absence. I feel their encouragement and grace as the presence of God. Still, I miss the warmth of my hand in yours. I long for the familiar rhythm of our Sunday mornings.

———◊———

How have you experienced God's presence amidst the
life changes following the death of your loved one?

Coming Home

Not so long ago, I'd open the door from the garage and hear you calling from your office, "How was your afternoon?" Like clockwork, your voice would greet me before I could even walk down the hall to find you swiveling around in your chair to face me.

These days, I open the door to silence. There's only the occasional ice dump from the ice maker to break the quiet. These are moments when the house feels especially lifeless and still. I miss your voice. I miss your attention to what's going on in my life. I miss our back-and-forth quips about the mundane things of life. I miss your laughter.

As I reach for the remote to turn on some background music, I glance at a photo scrolling through a digital frame the kids gave us for Christmas. There's your face beaming at me, so full of life and joy. I weep as I give thanks, even in the silence.

———◊———

How has silence impacted your journey through grief?

Donating Clothes

Purging the closet is an annual task that would normally take less than an hour. I would yank clothes from hangers and stuff them into a bag to take to the donation drop-off. But this was no ordinary closet-purging day. These were your clothes. Your plaid shirts and khaki pants. Your blue blazers and button-down oxford shirts. Your belts and socks. I folded them neatly and placed them gently, even reverently, into the bags. It was a slow, painful process that emotionally swept across all seasons of the year—from your summer T-shirts to silly holiday ties and your time-worn leather jackets.

I was struck by the way some things caused an immediate flashback. I could visualize you wearing that lightweight gray sweater at the lodge in South Africa. That tropical shirt was the one you wore while napping in a lounge chair in the shade on our favorite beach in the Virgin Islands. Now I wonder, how can I just casually bundle up the memories and drop them off at the donation box?

———◊———

What has been your experience in dealing with the personal items of your loved one? How have you decided what to keep and what to donate?

Medical Building

Sometimes unexpected things trigger an emotional landslide.

Yesterday I had a routine doctor's appointment for the first time since you died. I went to the office in a medical complex where I'd been many times before. This time, though, I felt a wave of anxiety rush over me. The whooshing of the blood pressure cuff took me right back to the hospital room where I sat with you just days before you died at home. Waiting in the lab for my blood work ushered in memories of the countless pokes and prods you had experienced without either one of us realizing those were your last days.

When my doctor finally came into the exam room, she offered a hug and compassionate words. I collapsed into the warmth of her embrace.

———◊———

What has unexpectedly triggered a difficult memory for you?

Wedding Ring

On the day we were married, we gave each other matching wedding bands: wide, hammered-gold rings. They were classic, simple and sturdy. Through the decades that followed, neither of us took off our ring unless we were required to do so for a medical procedure. Even then, we knew that removing our wedding band was just a temporary measure. As we aged, we laughed about needing a slathering of soap to ease the ring over our arthritic knuckles. I don't remember either of us ever misplacing our ring because we so rarely took it off.

It wasn't long ago that you were looking closely at our hands as we sat side by side. You commented on how the decades had changed the hammered texture of our wedding bands so that now they were smooth and shiny. It was as if life had polished our rings in a slow-motion rock tumbler.

When the funeral home returned your ring to me following your death, I placed it in a drawstring bag and put it in my drawer. Though we vowed *'til death do us part*, I will continue to wear my ring. Love outlives death.

———◇———

What have you done with your wedding ring in the aftermath of the death of your loved one? Be confident in knowing there is no wrong answer.

Solo Photo

There is a photo of me sitting on a boulder with the Teton Mountains in the background. A single glance reminds me that you are no longer on the other side of the camera. "Stand over there. I want to take your photo," you would say when it was just the two of us on a trip. With no one around to take a photo of the two of us together, you'd position me in front of a special scene and snap an image. Occasionally we'd try a selfie, but we usually deemed them unflattering and deleted our fumbled attempts. You were always there with your eyes focused on me. But now you are gone. I dearly love other family members who step in as photographers and travel mates now, but I wrestle with the reality that they are not you.

———◊———

How have you experienced aloneness in this season of grief?

Office

Cleaning out your office has been surprisingly difficult—more emotionally draining than sorting through your clothes or discarding items from your bathroom drawers. Perhaps it's because I was often in those other spaces, putting away clean laundry or setting out new tubes of toothpaste. But your office was your private space where you conducted business, made phone calls, and highlighted passages in books you were reading. When I open the top drawer of your desk, I feel a strange twinge of guilt, as if I am invading your personal space. I am confident we didn't keep important secrets from each other, but I wonder if there were things you wished you could have tossed out if only you'd have known you were going to die soon.

Above your desk are shelves filled with awards and certificates of achievement and service that you received through the years. There's a wall calendar that has remained unturned since your death. My eyes are drawn to a whiteboard mounted on the wall with columns of words penned in your handwriting. What prompted you to write words like *persistence*, *integrity*, and *joy*? I wonder what I am to do with these treasured remnants of your life.

———◊———

When have you felt like you were invading the privacy of your loved one who has died?

Widow's Club

I never wanted to join the Widow's Club. Membership automatically came the moment you took your last breath.

For the first time in my life, I am living by myself. There's no sibling to share my room. No roommate or child still living at home. Not even a pet. As we both aged, I'd had fleeting thoughts of what life might be like if you were to die before me. Still, I never allowed those images to take root in my mind. They were more like butterflies that rest lightly on a flower for a brief second before flitting away. Thoughts of living without you were too raw, too painful. Yet now they are real.

Oh, how I wish I could somehow cancel my membership in this club for widows.

———◊———

How does being labeled as a widow or
widower make you uncomfortable?

Deflated Joy

Today it feels as though an industrial vacuum-seal machine has sucked the joy out of my life. It is as if the air has been pulled out, causing my joy to collapse and shrink around what's left of me. Simple things that once brought delight to ordinary days just don't any-more: Sunday brunches on the shady deck of a neigh-borhood restaurant, summertime outings to the peach orchard, spontaneous getaways to see changing leaves in the fall, and trips to the city to attend a concert. Our ordinary days were infused with joy—shared joy. And now that joy is so hard to find.

———◊———

In what ways have you experienced joylessness
following the death of your loved one?

Selling a Car

You knew I had an aversion to buying and selling cars. I've never been fascinated by the latest makes and models, and I certainly wasn't comfortable with wheeling and dealing for the best price. You laughed when I described a vehicle by its most basic attributes, like a silver SUV or a red sedan. However, whenever it was time to buy a new car, you always asked me for my input, saying you never wanted to make an important decision without me. Each time, I assured you that I had only two requirements for a new car: that it was safe and that it wasn't metallic pea green or neon yellow.

Not long after you died, I went to the garage to check the odometer and record the mileage for each of our vehicles since I knew it would be best to sell one. Except for the color, our cars were identical and were purchased on the same day. As I had assumed, mine had the greater mileage since it's the one we took on road trips. Thoughts of getting my car detailed,

negotiating with strangers, and handling the paperwork made my stomach churn. I felt so inexperienced,
even at my ripe age. I feared there would be questions for which I had no answers. My mind jumped to
thoughts of potential buyers poised to take advantage
of a naïve widow.

Then I thought about your friend who regularly
deals with buying and selling luxury cars. Although my
car wasn't in the luxury category, I hoped he might be
willing to guide me through the process. Taking a big
gulp of courage, I picked up the phone and asked for
help.

———◇———

What is something that you could ask a
knowledgeable friend to help you with?

Trash Day

It's Trash Day, and I am still in my pajamas.

Since the day we married, you have taken out the garbage on Monday mornings like clockwork. You hauled out the bulky bags and bins to the curb, never once complaining. Now it's up to me to remember that it's Trash Day or Recycling Day. I'm responsible for getting dressed in the early hours and strong-arming the recycling bin or bags. I know I sometimes told you "thank you," but now I wonder if I did it often enough. Did I remember to say "thank you" for all those selfless acts of love and service?

Today I will give thanks for your life as I roll the recycling bin to the curb.

————◊————

What selfless acts of love did your loved one do that you wish you could thank him/her for even now?

Texting

We had fun in this life, you and I. Comfortable fun that came easily when the kids were grown and it was just the two of us left to entertain each other. I think back to the times when I'd be working on my laptop and was interrupted by the whoosh of your text coming in on my phone with a familiar question: *Whatcha doing?* You were just steps away down the hall. I was within easy earshot, but you chose to text instead of shout because it made both of us smile.

I miss those texts about ordinary life. Today I scrolled through my phone to read the texts you sent me during the last few months. As if on cue, my eyes spilled warm tears. Oh, how I miss knowing that you are just down the hall.

———◇———

What is something ordinary, even silly, that
you miss about your loved one?

Accordion

There's one thing I've learned since you died: Grief is like an accordion. There are times I want to pull open the bellows and force air into my weary being, so I volunteer to help with a mission project at church. I join friends for lunch and let their kindness both distract and fill me. I take a short trip with the kids and grandkids and bask in their laughter. I can feel my life expand.

Then there comes a moment when being with people starts to feel overwhelming. Conversation becomes tedious and siphons my energy. Sadness presses down and compresses my spirit. Suddenly, I am desperate to retreat to solitude. I want to put on my pajamas and escape the noise and the normalcy of other people's lives. Like an accordion, it's back and forth, in and out. Expand and compress.

————◊————

Have you experienced a similar rhythm of grief? Is there an image like an accordion that helps you think about grief?

A Different Kind of Grief

Your death hit me differently than the death of my elderly parents. Though their deaths were no less significant to me, what I am experiencing now in the aftermath of your death feels different.

Maybe it was because your death was more unexpected and I had less time to prepare for it. I had journeyed alongside my beloved parents as they dealt with the difficult transitions of late life. I watched them struggle with health challenges and losses that come with a very long life.

Maybe it's because you were still alive when my parents died. You were right beside me as we buried them and in the days that followed. You loved them every bit as much as I did and grieved alongside me. In mourning them, I felt a sense of relief knowing they no longer had physical struggles. But despite the tears and sadness that came with their deaths, I did not feel as alone as I do now. Your death has left me feeling

more disoriented and more vulnerable as I try to adapt
to this new normal without you in my life.

———◊———

*How have you experienced the death of your spouse differently
from the deaths of other family members or close friends?*

Sleeping

Where do I sleep now that you have died and I am alone? Do I sleep on my normal side of the bed? Do I try to move to the middle? I can't even imagine sleeping on your side; your book and your clock still rest on your nightstand. Somehow it seems wrong, I think. I suppose it is a little thing in the big scheme of life, but it's also disorienting after years of a nightly routine. There hasn't been time enough to create a new habit.

Tonight, I will be gentle with myself. I will try to drift off to sleep on the sofa, watching a feel-good movie. There will be time enough to figure out my new normal.

———◊———

How has grief changed your sleeping habits?

Wedding Dance

It's the first wedding I've attended since you died. It feels so odd, being single and seated at a reception table with married people who graciously make every effort to include me in the conversation. The music starts and couples move across the dance floor. And then it happens—a romantic slow tune you loved so much. I can picture you getting up from your chair and grabbing my hand to lead me out to the dance floor.

Instead, I sit quietly in the flickering candlelight among the lush floral arrangements and dab my eyes with the linen napkin. In this lifetime, there will not be another slow dance with you. You will never twirl me or dip me with that impish grin on your face again. Those days are forever gone except in my memory.

———◊———

What has caused you to mourn the loss of romance?

Voicemail

I've dreaded doing this for so long, but I knew it was time. I went to my cell phone and found the voice-mails you had left me over the past few months. I knew that hearing your voice again would unleash an emotional surge, but I was not prepared to hear you say in a sweet, upbeat voice, "Call me when you can so I can hear your voice." Immediately, I began to sob from the deepest place in my spirit.

The message was not what I had expected. It was not a reminder to get stamps at the post office or an update that you were meeting a client at 3 p.m. Instead, it was a tender search for connection with me: you wanted to hear my voice. It was a stark reminder that I would never hear your voice again.

Finally, I lifted myself from the sofa but continued with a guttural cry as I turned on the shower and let the water run over me as if it could somehow wash away the agony. How could a voicemail bring such pain and comfort at the same time?

I thought back to the day that you left that message and realized I had been on an overnight trip for a speaking event. How could you have known that I would listen to your words again and again after you were gone? While I am so thankful for the recording, the idea that I will never hear you speak again in this lifetime has left me wrecked.

———◊———

Have you listened to the voicemail messages left by your loved one? What was your experience?

No More a Twosome

Yesterday I drove fifteen miles to a nearby town to avoid eating in a local restaurant by myself. At that moment, I just didn't want to be the topic of the whispered conversation of people who knew me and pitied my new role in life. I didn't want to talk about how I am doing after your death. I just wanted an enchilada.

It was a spontaneous decision with no time to coordinate meeting a friend. It was also a blunt reminder that I am no longer part of a twosome. You and I often went out to eat together. We sat across from each other in restaurant booths and in seats B and C on the airplane. Our knees brushed against each other under the Sunday school table. We walked down the church aisle to take Communion together. We brushed our teeth beside each other and shared a closet. Now I am a one in a twosome world.

Just a few days ago, I encountered a husband and wife having an animated argument while grocery shopping. They were belittling each other with sharp words. I desperately wanted to pull them aside and whisper, "Please don't squander what time you have together. Don't miss the chance to cheer each other on instead of chewing each other out. Don't let a trivial argument steal precious time. It will be gone too soon."

———◊———

*How have you tried to escape the pressure
of being one in a twosome world?*

Syncing Calendars

Every few weeks, you would make an announcement: "Get your calendar and let's sync up." Though you kept your schedule on your digital devices, I still preferred a paper calendar, so we would sit together and sift through our personal, business, and ministry schedules for the next few weeks or months to make sure we were each aware of the other's upcoming meetings, medical appointments, podcast interviews, and speaking events.

On the day you died, our calendars were chock-full of upcoming events: an out-of-state ministry trip for me, Zoom meetings and real estate closings for you. Suddenly, everything came to a screeching halt as I turned my attention to planning your celebration of life service and coordinating family travel plans.

Everything in my life stopped, but that was not the case for others. On the day you died, neighbors still took out the trash and got snagged in traffic as they drove across the lake to the city. People celebrated birthdays and anniversaries, even as I made calls to loved ones, barely squeaking out the words, "He died." Now I scroll through social media and see photos of your business colleagues celebrating awards, but you are not there. I see memories pop up on the screen reminding me of what you were doing on that calendar date a year or five years before.

Grief is not linear. It cannot be scheduled on the calendar. And it cannot be bypassed by turning the calendar to a new page.

————◊————

How has the death of your loved one changed your calendar life?

Unfulfilled Dreams

I opened the fireproof security box to put away some papers and saw our passports on top of other papers. We had recently renewed them, and they were stored in a plastic bag along with our global entry documents that we hoped would make international travel as easy as possible.

We had a dream to take the kids and grandkids to our favorite resort in the Caribbean once it had been rebuilt following the hurricane damage. We wanted them to experience the turquoise water and the tree-lined white crescent beaches that we raved about so much. We had also pondered a trip to visit our daughter in Europe, despite concerns about arthritic knees and long overseas flights. But like so many other things, these are dreams that will never be fulfilled. We will not sit together and applaud as our grandkids graduate from high school. We will not dance together at their weddings nor take that European riverboat cruise. Those dreams will go unfulfilled.

Although I could still make those trips by myself, I know it wouldn't be the same. The dream of doing things together has vanished. I am left to wonder if the happy places of our past will ever bring happiness again now that you are gone.

———◊———

What dreams did you and your loved one
share that will go unfulfilled?

Technology

Technology has a strange intersection with death. Not long ago, family and friends would have phoned people to share the news of your death. But on the morning you died, most people found out by a text, an email, or a social media post. Even before the funeral director had left our house, my phone was abuzz with sympathy texts. In truth, replying to those texts from friends was less stressful than repeatedly choking back tears in a series of phone conversations.

Yet I have also discovered that your digital afterlife poses a disturbing challenge. Though you are gone from this earth, your online presence has not disappeared. Voicemails and texts still pile up as the kids and I wait to permanently turn off your phone until we are confident that we have retrieved all the information we might need. For weeks after your death, emails continued to flood your computer. Updated passwords had to be found. Accounts had to be closed or transferred to my name. Instead of imagining you

gathered above with the saints in that cloud of wit-
nesses, I keep thinking about your digital cloud.

Soon after your death, I asked our kids to remove
your Facebook page so that your upcoming birthday
notification would not circulate through your social
media friends. It's so unsettling to see people post
happy birthday wishes to someone who has died. Even
now, memories with you from my own social media
pages pop up and catch me off guard. Sometimes the
photos make me smile; other times, they feel like a gut
punch. Technology has certainly changed the world. I
just never expected it to change the way I grieve.

———◊———

What have been your experiences with technology and grief?

Guilt

For some reason, my mind keeps wandering back to the last few days of your life. I wish I could easily redirect my thoughts away from the painful images of death and loss, but like a river that cannot be controlled, my mind demands its own way. So, today I have decided to let my thoughts meander to places I'd rather not go. I will let hurt and guilt spill over the banks, knowing the pain will recede in time.

Though you had been in and out of the hospital over the span of two weeks, I don't think either of us knew that your death was so close. If you had those inner thoughts, you didn't verbalize them. It seemed we were both focused on a plan to return you to good health. Now that you are gone, I wonder if I did all I could have done to be the best caregiver and wife you deserved. Did I do the right things? Did I ask the right questions of the medical staff? Did I speak to you with utmost compassion and love? I know I tried, but certainly I could have done more.

Maybe I should have spent every night in the chair at your bedside instead of sleeping in a hotel a few blocks away from the hospital. Maybe I should have demanded one more test or one more answer. There is a strong undercurrent of *what ifs* in the wanderings of my mind. It is like an estuary where freshwater mixes with salt water from the ocean tide. In this brackish water of my mind, guilt intermingles with grief. Then I pause and remember the character of the man I knew you to be. A man who would have extended grace and forgiveness.

———◊———

In what ways do you feel guilty about the loss of your loved one? Are you offering yourself grace and forgiveness?

Garage

Almost every day I walk into the garage with good intentions to straighten it up and sweep it out. But instead, I close the door and convince myself that I'll get to it later. Like so many things in life, the garage was immaculate and well-organized when we first moved in. Over time, things accumulated, and the garage became a little more disorganized. There are swim noodles draped from a hook on the wall and a car seat for the youngest grandchild stacked on a tub of outdoor Christmas lights. There's an extra Christmas tree left from staging a home during the holidays. There are paint cans and gardening tools, a wheelbarrow, and a fertilizer spreader, even though a landscape company does the yard maintenance now.

The garage was your territory. Everywhere I look, there are reminders of you. You never liked the garage to be messy and you talked about your plan for reorganizing it, but then you died. Now I'm not sure what to donate. What things might I need in the future?

What do I do with your old personalized real estate signs or your oversized tool cabinet? For now, I will walk around the clutter until my heart is ready.

————◊————

In what ways has disarray impacted you in the days following the death of your loved one?

Magical Moments

Early this morning, a series of images drifted through my hazy mind while the world was still asleep. It was like a dream, only better, because these moving images captured magical moments that had occurred in our life together. In one scene, we were dancing under a canopy of white lights at our son's wedding reception in the Texas Hill Country. In another, you were giving the toast at our daughter's wedding in a California vineyard. Then you were laughing with our younger daughter in a twilight moment at a Central Park restaurant where we were celebrating her new career adventure. There were other images of when we were the only two people on a sugar-white beach, of when we took turns cradling a newborn grandchild for the first time, of when we gathered with all the family around a table in a magnificent log house in Utah to celebrate your birthday.

Life is made up of countless ordinary days that are punctuated by magical moments of pure bliss. Those magical moments seem so perfect, you wonder how life could possibly get better. Now that you are gone, I wonder if I will have any more of those extra special moments. Hope and faith tell me I will, but it's difficult to imagine those moments without seeing the magic reflected in your eyes.

———◊———

What are the magical moments from your life together
that you would make into a video if you could?

Kids and Grandkids

The other morning, I texted our adult kids and told them that I would not be answering my phone that day. I didn't want them to be alarmed if they called and I didn't respond. They have each been so loving and supportive throughout this difficult season following your death, and they are dealing with their own grief too. You would be so proud of their attentiveness. They faithfully check on me; they call and send fun videos of the grandkids. They graciously invite me to come along on their trips. The older grandkids text me sweet notes, and the youngest one FaceTimes me, but being separated by hundreds, even thousands, of miles has been hard.

Still, on this Saturday morning, I didn't want to talk to anyone. Even before the sun came up, I realized it was going to be one of *those* days. A memory had unexpectedly unleashed my tears. Instead of pushing back, I texted the kids and announced, *I'm okay, but I wanted you to know that it's a raw kind of day where I can't talk without crying, so I don't want to try.* I didn't want to respond to phone calls or texts, or even cute videos of our grandson throwing rocks in the river. I just felt the need to sit alone in my grief and be miserable for a while, so I did.

I stayed in my lounging clothes all day and let my emotions have their way. When I passed by a mirror, I flinched at my puffy face and swollen eyes. My nose was so stopped-up, I could barely breathe except through my mouth. By the time late afternoon came, I was emotionally drained, but I realized that I felt better. I felt lighter and brighter. Sometimes hope comes wrapped in tears.

———◊———

How have you given into a raw day into your life? What was the outcome?

If I Had Known

If I had known that day was going to be your last, I would have fought through the sobs to tell you one last time how much I loved being your wife and best friend in this earthly life. I would have snuggled with you longer and whispered how much I admired your integrity, your selflessness, and your tenderness. Our kids and grandkids would have gathered around and hugged you mightily as they thanked you for being such a faithful father and grandfather. With breaking hearts, we would have cried while sharing stories, but we would have laughed too. I would have served coconut pie and played your favorite tunes from the 1950s while we danced barefoot in the kitchen one last time. As we felt those final moments slipping away, I would have tried my best to audibly voice a prayer of gratitude to God for helping us find each other those many years ago. Threading your fingers through mine, we would have just sat together, holding hands. Through tear-streaked faces, I think we would have smiled and kissed each other goodbye, knowing we will embrace each other again on the other side.

———◊———

How would you complete the sentence:
If I had known, _____?

Part III

Grief Through the Year

New Year's Day

The new year comes with hopeful expectations of a fresh start, but this year is a new beginning that I never wanted. The clock will move forward, but my heart will not. How can I be happy about a new year that you will never know?

With a few exceptions, we stayed home on New Year's Eve. Neither of us enjoyed late-night parties or navigating highways with partygoers who'd had too much to drink. In our empty-nest season, we usually celebrated with a party-for-two in front of the fireplace. We were content to wear obligatory party hats and quietly toast the New Year by ourselves. Then if we were able to stay awake, we'd watch TV to see the ball drop in New York City. New Year's Day was typically filled with football and parades. You weren't a huge fan of black-eyed peas, a New Year's tradition from my Texas roots. However, you would gladly eat them for good luck if I put them in a nine-bean soup served with hot cornbread and butter.

This year, there will be no pot of soup, no black-eyed peas. It feels like my luck ran out last year on the day you died. And besides, a big pot of soup would be a waste. There will be no party hats, glittery clothes, or thoughtful resolutions. I will get through it, but I just can't conjure up enthusiasm for the start of a new year when I will be living it without you.

—————◊—————

What are your feelings about celebrating the New Year's holiday now that your loved one has died?

Gray Days of Winter

You knew how much I disliked gray winter days, especially when they stacked up in succession like a long row of dominos waiting for someone to topple the first one. More than once, you heard me grumble that days without sunshine are hard on my psyche. Now I realize that grieving your death in winter feels like a double burden.

In these early months of the year, the world seems unwelcoming. The cheery holiday lights are gone, and the landscape is painted in shades of grief—fog, smoke, pewter, and slate. Leafless trees are dark silhouettes against the gray background. Other than a few struggling yellow pansies, there are no colorful signs of life in view. No wonder it's so easy to feel sad.

Television newscasters warn about the dangers of flu and respiratory infections. The meteorologist predicts a winter storm, and I begin to make a mental list of all the things you would do in preparation of the possibility of frozen pipes or an electrical outage.

Today my life feels coated in thick ice that causes tree limbs to groan and break.

I will surrender to winter's grip. I will hibernate and pull the hoodie up over my unbrushed hair. Maybe I will make a cup of your favorite hot chocolate and hold it in both hands to feel the warmth like you often did. By late afternoon though, I promise to step outside and breathe in the fresh air. I will fill the depths of my lungs and let the chill of winter brush across my face before going back inside. I know that in this deep grief and loneliness, you would remind me that spring will return.

———◊———

How has winter impacted your journey of grief?

Valentine's Day

As much as I would like to pretend that February 14 is just an ordinary day, television and social media ads make it impossible. Before the Christmas tinsel is packed away, Valentine's Day commercials for flowers, chocolate, and jewelry begin. In one ad, a dreamy-eyed woman gasps in surprise when her young man opens a ring box and drops to his knee. In another, a lovestruck man and woman sway to the music on a city rooftop bathed in candlelight. My favorite ad ends with an older couple walking down a sidewalk, arm in arm.

Now that you are gone, how am I supposed to get excited about a day that features couples in love? I'm aware that Valentine's Day commercials are intended to manipulate my emotions, and they do. Each is a painful reminder of what I lost when you died. Maybe there should be a line of Valentine cards that features hearts with huge cracks down the middle, hearts crushed into a million pieces, or heart-shaped balloons that drift into the sky after escaping a loved one's grip.

Someone recently told me that I should think of Valentine's Day as a day to celebrate all kinds of love, not just romantic love. In my head, I know that's true, but it's hard to overcome the tender images that swirl in my imagination. So today I will take a Valentine tea party to an older friend who has been widowed for over two decades. We will sit in her nursing home room and celebrate just how lucky-in-love we once were.

————◊————

What are your feelings about romantic love in this season of loss? How do you plan to spend Valentine's Day this year?

Ash Wednesday

Tonight, our pastor dipped his finger in the small pot of ashes and drew death on my forehead. It was gritty and gray, another reminder that you, my beloved, are dead. Your body is now ashes, and one day, mine will be too. There's just no escaping the reality of Ash Wednesday. It's all about death and dying. *We are dust and to dust we shall return.*

Recently, I heard friends discussing what they planned to give up during Lent as a symbol of self-sacrifice. A few are giving up sugar or desserts. One is staying off social media for the next forty days. Another is sacrificing her morning coffee. But when I ponder the question for myself, I am struck by the magnitude of what I've already given up—you. I didn't want to sacrifice you, but I had no choice. I wonder how giving up a morning caffeine fix compares to giving up the love of your life. Suddenly my mind is overwhelmed with the thought of God's sacrifice. Perhaps

Ash Wednesday, like grief, is a necessary step toward healing and wholeness.

———◊———

How are you intentionally embracing the pain of grief to move forward?

Tax Day

They say that nothing is certain except death and taxes. That seems especially true today. You were the financial guy, a corporate controller in your first career. You loved numbers, and I loved words. It is not surprising that you handled all the details of filing our taxes. Beginning in January, you commanded the dining room table as a sorting station for piles of papers and receipts. Later, you spent hours at your laptop before you printed the final document, which you then tried to explain to me before having me sign on the dotted line.

Then you were gone, leaving behind a drawerful of papers and receipts and a pocket calendar documenting your business mileage. Filing paperwork for income taxes was in your wheelhouse, not mine. Even the lingo is unfamiliar and intimidating to me. But I have no choice but to learn it or to get help.

Your death has uncovered things I did not know I did not know. There are times I feel overwhelmed by my own inexperience. However, I am learning that it's okay to lean on others' expertise and assistance. Today I called a local CPA and hauled a box of paperwork to his office. I feel better already, just knowing I'm not stuck.

———◇———

How has the death of your loved one uncovered things you did not know you did not know?

Good Friday to Easter

I told myself that I needed to attend the Good Friday service at church. I have often said that you can't fully experience the joy of Easter morning without first experiencing Jesus' suffering at the crucifixion. I still believe that truth. This year is different though, and I toyed with the idea of using grief as an excuse to stay home. But I went to the Good Friday service anyway. I sat in the darkened sanctuary for the Tenebrae service and felt my inner light diminish as each candle was extinguished. When the service concluded, we were asked to leave in silence. Actually, it was a relief. I was grateful not to have to talk to another human being on the way to the parking lot.

These weeks leading to Easter have been an emotional mash-up. My mind has been flooded with images of death and the crucifixion along with baby chicks and candy-filled Easter baskets. I forced myself to decorate the dining room table with my collection of bird nests, each cradling pale blue speckled eggs. I displayed the tall, decorative rabbits on the front porch, just as I have done in years past. I went through all the motions and emotions of preparing for Easter. Then Sunday morning arrived. The sanctuary was filled with lilies. Children came in their shiny new shoes and pastel clothes. People hugged and gave "Happy Easter" blessings. The trumpets and tympani played, the choir sang, and the Resurrection story was joyously proclaimed.

My heart felt as empty as the tomb. Joy will come again, I know. But for now, I must trust the Resurrection story *because He lives.*

———◊———

How have you navigated Holy Week now that your loved one is gone? What feelings does Easter spark in you this year?

Mother's Day

I told the kids and grandkids that I would be fine. They are scattered across the globe, and I was confident that I could muddle through this Mother's Day without them since I would be seeing them in less than a month. Still, walking the halls of church without you by my side was hard, especially on this day that celebrates the love of family.

In the days leading up to Mother's Day, I decided to host my own little pity party after church to avoid the lunch crowds and stares. I ordered a steak dinner, including a loaded baked potato, a small loaf of warm bread, and dessert to be delivered to the house. It was my way of drowning my loneliness in comfort food. When the delivery person handed me the big brown bag, he smiled and wished me a very Happy Mother's Day. I thanked him, then I closed the door and cried.

Throughout the afternoon, there were FaceTime calls with the kids and grandkids, each from a different time zone. By the time the last one called, I was emotionally weary. What began as a cheery conversation dissolved into a puddle of tears as I fought a tightened throat to make my words audible. I was both frustrated by my emotions yet grateful for my family's tender love and compassion. As I hung up from the last phone call, I felt a sense of relief and decided to celebrate the fact that I had managed to get through another difficult special occasion on this grief journey. I finished off the key lime pie.

————◊————

Has Mother's Day triggered an emotional
avalanche for you? If so, how?

Father's Day

What do you do when it is Father's Day and both your husband and your father have died and the fathers of your grandchildren live in other cities? It's the first time in my life I've not had a father in my family to celebrate in person. It seems another residue of death.

A week before Father's Day, I decided to be proactive so I wouldn't be left in a quandary when Sunday finally arrived. I invited two longtime friends over for Sunday lunch. They too are widows who are just ahead of me on the journey through grief. I set the table for three. Our adult children sent a lovely floral arrangement for the table. I ordered salad trios and dessert from a favorite take-out restaurant because I didn't want to cook. I asked one friend to offer grace because I still struggle to get through a prayer without weeping.

Our Father's Day lunch was simple and uncomplicated. We ate. We reminisced about our loved ones. We hugged goodbye and got a little emotional. By

mid-afternoon, my phone was ringing. Instead of calling their dad to wish him Happy Father's Day, my
children were calling to check on me. I told them I
got through it.

———◊———

How have you planned ahead to celebrate a special
occasion? Have you given yourself permission
to keep things simple and uncomplicated?

Fourth of July

During the last fifteen years or so, our hometown Fourth of July parade became our empty-nesters' tradition. With our children and grandchildren scattered, it was usually just the two of us to celebrate Independence Day. On the morning of the Fourth, we dressed in red, white, and blue and drove to the nearby parade route, positioning our folding chairs in a spot of shade on the same corner every year. It's where we sat for both the Fourth of July parade and the Christmas parade. Local civic leaders, regular parade participants, and friends knew our spot and always gave us a special wave and greeting. Then as the final parade entrant passed by, we'd avoid the crowd by taking a back way home, where you'd fire up the grill for our celebratory lunch.

Now that it's just me, I find myself facing a dilemma. Do I go solo to the parade this year and steel myself for the uncomfortable looks of sympathy from caring passers-by? Do I ask a friend to go and sit in your place? Do I avoid the parade this year and wait until dark, celebrating privately on my own porch when the city's fireworks show begins? Or is this the year I should travel somewhere and do something totally different? Sometimes there aren't any good answers.

————◊————

How have you experienced a dilemma involving a holiday tradition now that your loved one is gone?

Swimming

When we downsized more than a decade ago, we left behind the backyard swimming pool where our family spent countless hours on summer evenings. We exchanged our two-story home and acre lot overlooking the lake for a new, smaller home with an HOA community pool. As much as we loved our big house, we both were relieved to have fewer maintenance concerns as we grew older.

In these empty-nest years, we often grabbed our beach towels and pool noodles and headed to the community pool first thing in the morning. We would sink into the cool water before the sun drilled down on the day. Almost always, it was just the two of us at that early hour. Although we did some laps for exercise, we really went to the pool just to float and talk.

Since you died, I have not been to the community pool. Not even once. Sometimes I think about it as I drive by and see it empty. It's strange how something I once loved to do now holds such little appeal. Maybe before the hot days of summer are over, I will go and submerge myself in the clear blue water. Maybe I will float in the waters of grief and just breathe. Or maybe I won't. I haven't decided yet.

———◊———

How have you stepped away from a tradition during this season of grief?

First Fire of the Season

The day is finally here but there is little to celebrate. It's the day I get to light the first fire of the autumn season. After long, sweltering summers, we always looked forward to the changing seasons. You would watch the skies for the first flock of geese migrating south. When the temperature finally dipped into the low fifties, it was officially cool enough to have an early-morning fire in the fireplace, even if it was just until the sun warmed things up again.

Back when we built our empty-nester home, we chose a fireplace with gas logs so that it would be convenient to start a fire on a whim. Sure, we missed the aroma of a real wood fire, but neither of us missed hauling in the logs or cleaning out the ashes. The simplicity of a no-fuss fire made it perfect for us in this stage of life.

Today as I look around the living room, everything seems the same as in years past. The family tartan blanket is draped across the bench. The hand-turned wooden bowl is filled with creamy dried hydrangeas from our yard. A garland of autumn leaves is draped across the stone fireplace and there is a pumpkin on the hearth. The room is decorated, but it seems bare. You are not here to share in the ritual of the changing seasons. As I start the fire with a single click, I sit back with a hollow heart and moist eyes to watch the flames dance. It's a difficult truth in this tender season when falling leaves signal that winter is coming. Life includes death.

———◊———

What about autumn has been difficult for you this year? Are there ways in which the changing seasons have brought you comfort?

Football Games

The familiar opening song of Game Day jars me unexpectedly and triggers memories of past football seasons. You and I enjoyed cheering our favorite college and professional teams together at home. In fact, watching weekend football was part of the rhythm of autumn, like making a pot of stew and a loaf of homemade bread. Now I am slumped down on the sofa by myself, watching the players with familiar jerseys on the television screen. As I often do these days, I let out a sigh. There's no need for me to shout down the hall to remind you that the kick-off is just minutes away. You are not there. It's such a strange feeling when I remember there's no one to clap alongside me when our team scores a touchdown. There's no one to groan about the interception or to share nachos. It's just me trying to integrate grief into this football season.

————◊————

How has grief been an interruption to the
natural rhythm of autumn?

Halloween

Driving through our community reminds me that Halloween often plays mean tricks on a grieving heart. There are skeletons sitting in rocking chairs and grave- stones planted in flower beds. Just a few blocks away, there is a front-yard spectacle of coffins, vampires, and the Grim Reaper wielding his bloody scythe. Every- where I look, it seems, there are inescapable images of death and decay on full display, even nestled among friendly scarecrows and smiling jack-o-lanterns.

When our kids were young, Halloween was a fun time of making costumes, carving pumpkins, and trick- or-treating. You accompanied the kids to neighbors' houses while I stayed home and handed out candy to other trick-or-treaters. Through the years, our roles shifted. I still stuffed the treat bags with your favor- ite candy bars in case there were leftovers, but you became the host on Halloween evening. From your office, you could hear the voices of children coming up the steps to the front door. You'd grab the candy basket and open the door just as they shouted, "Trick-or-treat!" I sat back on the sofa and listened as you commented on the children's unique costumes.

Now that Halloween is just a day away, I find myself in a tug-of-war of ambivalent emotions. The truth is, I just don't feel very playful this year. The thought of cheerily answering the door to even the cutest trick-or-treaters seems more daunting than joyful. However, I don't want to become a grumpy recluse in a darkened house. This year, I think I will resist the pressure to play a jovial host. Instead, I will place a big basket filled with treat bags on the well-lit porch along with a sign: *Please take one bag so there's plenty for all.* Then before the first trick-or-treaters arrive, I will go to a back room in the house to watch a feel-good movie and hope that the princesses and pirates will somehow understand.

————◊————

How has the celebration of Halloween impacted your grief journey? Has it caused you to think more about death and the afterlife?

All Saints' Day

It's chilly and rainy this Sunday morning. Not even the aroma of freshly baked pumpkin muffins and coffee could lift my spirits today. The weather seems an appropriate backdrop to this day that I've dreaded for a while. On All Saints' Day, we remember the people in our church family who have died during the last year. It is always a solemn and meaningful service, but today at church, I was devastated when I saw your photo fill the big screen. I heard the pastor read your name as your candle was lit and a bell tolled. Even knowing what to expect, I was overwhelmed by the stark reminder that you are gone.

Many years ago, when I was the chair of the worship council at church, I asked you to make a special banner for All Saints' Day. You built a tall T-shaped frame from thick dowel rods, and I attached long, wide white satin ribbons with small bells sewn to each ribbon's end, one for each person in our church family who had died during the year. When the prelude music stopped, the banner was carried into the sanctuary in total silence, interrupted only by the soft, tinkling sound of the bells. It always gave me goosebumps, remembering the saints who went before us.

Now you are one of those saints.

Though our church's rituals around All Saints' Day have changed through the years, I hold dear the sacred sound of those bells filling the silence. In fact, when you died, I gave each family member a small bell to ring as we recessed from the sanctuary into the narthex at your celebration of life service.

Today I drove home from church and put on my favorite jeans and sweatshirt. I sat in front of the fire and listened to the haunting melody of *Pie Jesu* as I reflected on how this day was both heartbreaking and comforting at once. It seemed God was trying to tell me something. *This, my beloved, is good grief.*

———◊———

If your church celebrates All Saints' Day, what feelings are you experiencing as the day grows near? In what ways are you living in the tension that could be described as good grief?

Turkey Baskets

As the Sunday morning reminder about the church's Turkey Basket effort scrolls across the worship screen, an unexpected wave of sadness washes over me. It is late October, but in my mind, the Turkey Basket effort marks the beginning of the holiday season.

For many years, you and I would shop together for all the suggested food items for an under-resourced family's Thanksgiving dinner. We would go to the store after church and check off every item on the list, then add some decorative napkins and fall decorations. Since we no longer shopped for our own Thanksgiving dinner, the idea of providing food for another family became a favorite tradition. Last year on the Monday before Thanksgiving, like in years past, you carried the heavy basket to the car and drove it to the church where youth volunteers loaded the baskets onto a truck destined for inner city families.

Now that you are gone, I find myself making mental excuses for not filling a turkey basket. *It's too heavy. It's too much trouble for one person. It's too emotionally triggering.* I'm not sure why buying the ingredients for a Thanksgiving meal seems so daunting this year. What do green beans, sweet potatoes, and a frozen turkey have to do with grief anyway? A lot, I'm learning. Gratefully, I discovered that monetary donations to assist in this project are welcomed. So, for this Thanksgiving, I am pressing pause on tradition. I will write a check for the Turkey Basket ministry instead. Next year, I will consider shopping again.

———◊———

As you ponder Thanksgiving Day without your loved one, how might you push pause on a tradition to give space for your grief?

Thanksgiving Day

You loved comfort food, so it is not surprising that Thanksgiving was a favorite day of the year for you. It was a food fest that provided joyous family conversation, football games, and leftovers to last for days.

When our kids were young, our home was the scene of Thanksgiving dinner with extended family. You cheered me on as I tried to perfect my grandmother's cornbread dressing. With holiday parades playing on the TV in the background, you helped clean the kitchen and light the candles before everyone arrived.

After our children had children of their own, our family discovered it was easier if we traveled to them since we had more time and fewer constraints. So we packed up and went to their homes to celebrate. Usually, we drove scenic back roads to our son's home in the Texas Hill Country, but last year we went to our daughter's home in California. On the night before Thanksgiving, we shared a unique family dinner with the kids and grandkids in a private, candlelit yurt in the wine country. Wherever we landed for Thanksgiving, we counted the blessing of just being together.

In my heart, I know that Thanksgiving and gratitude go together like pumpkin pie and whipped cream. There are countless things for which I am grateful this year, but your absence is not one of them. Grief is casting a long shadow over the entire holiday season. This morning, I am driving to our son's home. It is a lonely trip with too much time to think. I made a different dessert this year. I wish you were here to enjoy it. I will look around the table and will be grateful for the love in each face. However, my heart will need some time to catch up.

———◊———

What things are you grateful for even in this season of grief? How might your heart need time to catch up?

Christmas Stockings

Over the last decade, we simplified our holiday decorating scheme. We managed to pare down the decorations to what would fit in closets so you wouldn't have to navigate the attic stairs while carrying heavy tubs. Now my collection of caroler dolls and my folk-art nativity set are easily accessible on a shelf in my bedroom closet. The big red bows for the outside garlands hang in a hall closet. Mr. and Mrs. Santa are snuggled under the attic stairs, awaiting their time to flank the fireplace as they've done for over fifty years.

On the top shelf of my bedroom closet, there's a time-worn gift box that holds a dozen handmade Christmas stockings already strung on a long pre-measured silk cord. They are ready to hang above the fireplace as soon as Thanksgiving is over. As each child was born and each in-law was welcomed into the family, I handstitched and personalized another Christmas stocking with their name and added it to the length of silk cord. As our family grew through the years, I simply moved the stockings closer together. During the last fifteen years or so when we traveled to be with our extended family for Christmas, you helped me take down the stockings from our home so we could re-hang them at the vacation rental. Just a few weeks after you died, our daughter asked about the Christmas stockings. She wanted reassurance that your stocking would remain in the line of our family stockings this year, just as it had always been.

Today, I opened the lid to the box and caught a glimpse of your stocking on top of all the others. I fingered the thin, gold cord that formed your name. Tears trickled from my eyes as I lifted it up to hang above the fireplace. To borrow a phrase from a friend, it was one of those happy-sad moments.

————◊————

What happy-sad moments are you experiencing at Christmas?

Miniature Train

I still remember the Christmas Eve you received the miniature train set as a gift from my brother and sister-in-law. When they asked what they could get you that year, I had a spontaneous thought about a much-wanted gift you never received as a child. You were almost sixty, but your eyes danced like those of a six-year-old boy when you unwrapped the long box with the model train set. It was a great surprise! Each year you would spend an afternoon unboxing the railroad track and individual train cars and setting them up in the center of our long dining room table. Over time, you added miniature evergreen trees, quaint Victorian homes and store fronts, a post office, and a church. You were caught up in your own fantasy, and I watched the childlike joy on your face as you manned the controls to make the train chug through your winter village.

Now that Thanksgiving has passed, I have cleared away the pumpkins and autumn berries from the dining room table. The train set is still stored in your office closet, awaiting my decision. Do I set it up this year? It is such a tender reminder of your absence. Would setting up the train make me feel better or worse? Maybe I will just leave the box in your closet and wait for another Christmas when one of the grandkids might carry on the tradition. Grief is such an odd conundrum. Which Christmas traditions do I keep? Which ones do I discard, delay, or adapt? What new ones do I add?

———◊———

What Christmas traditions do you most associate with your loved one? What traditions do you plan to keep? What traditions will you change or discard? How will you decide?

Christmas Memories

I gave away our big Christmas tree and bought a more manageable tabletop tree. There was no way I could put up that tall tree by myself, and to be honest, I didn't even want to try. Likely, no one would notice if I didn't put up a tree this year, but the idea of no Christmas tree at all made me sad. So, I bought the small pre-lit tree, placed it on my grandmother's little table, plugged in the lights, and fluffed the branches. That's when I realized that the ornaments from the old tree were too large for this smaller tree. I briefly considered leaving the tree bare because that's how I feel. Then I had a spark of inspiration. I thought about the bells from your celebration of life service, the small bells our family rang as we walked the aisle at the end of the service. I hung the bells on the tree and smiled to myself, thinking about how much you loved Christmas.

When we married, you came with only a few holiday traditions of your own. Then I introduced you to my large and loving extended family with our litany of holiday traditions. After just one year of hosting the family festivities, you were all in for Christmas.

This week, I mailed out Christmas cards, but I had to include a statement about your death. I hung the stockings above the fireplace, but I had to hire someone to help me with hanging the greenery and red bows on the porch. Next week, I will make the pralines and the peanut butter balls, but I lament that you are not here to sneak one as you pass by. Everything about Christmas feels familiar yet terribly unfamiliar at the same time. The holiday music that used to make me sing in the car sometimes makes me cry. Putting up Christmas lights on the house seemed so joyful in years past, but now it feels like a chore. Christmas memories are everywhere this season, and that feels both comforting and unbearable.

———◊———

In what ways do Christmas memories bring you comfort in this season of grief? In what ways do they feel unbearable?

Family Circle

I have tried to brace myself for this Christmas Eve moment, but I knew it was a useless effort. Looking into the glistening eyes of our extended family gathered in a circle to pray and to sing "Silent Night" is full-force sensory overload. Even in past years when you were standing beside me, we often teared up as we passed the candlelight around the family circle. Tonight, you are not here to stand with me among the kids and grand-kids, the aunts and uncles and cousins. You are not here in your Christmas sweater and the holiday tissue paper crown from the holiday popper. Though it is painful, I desperately want and need to stand in this family cir-cle. Tonight we sing, though our voices break. We pass the light, though our hands quiver. It is a tradition that must continue. It is a teaching moment for the younger generations. As a family, we acknowledge our loss and give thanks to God for the Christ child. We laugh and we cry because we love one another so deeply.

———◊———

How are you intentionally embracing the pain this Christmas?

Our Wedding Anniversary

It's almost our anniversary, and I don't know where to go or what to do. In previous years, we always made a special date to visit "our tree"—an ancient oak tree with a large limb that bent toward the ground. Long ago, we married under that tree on the lawn of a historic estate overlooking an urban lake. You once described our wedding as simple, picturesque, and perfect, and I agree. Now I can't muster the motivation to return to our tree.

Through the decades, we talked about how the tree was a parallel to our aging lives. Each year, the limb bent a little lower to the ground until finally the arborists had to construct a brace to help support it. Even so, the tree remains gracious and welcoming.

For our anniversary this year, friends and family have offered to return with me to the tree. Not yet, I say. I'm not ready to see the beautiful old tree without you at my side. Instead, I'll spend the day looking back

through all the photos we took while visiting our tree
through the years. That's the best I can do this year.

————◊————

What was your anniversary tradition? How will
you plan to celebrate your wedding anniversary,
or do you prefer not to dwell on that date?

Your Birthday

Today is your birthday. I am alone at home with a cupcake and candle.

Though our friends and family graciously offered to be with me today, I chose to celebrate it by myself, doing things you loved. Maybe I am intentionally making it an emotionally difficult day, but somehow it feels right.

I began the day by making your favorite pecan waffles and bacon. I smiled as I poured a generous helping of maple syrup on top, like you always did. Then I silenced my phone and queued up your favorite movie, knowing the tears would spill every time I heard one of the lines you had memorized by watching it so many times. This afternoon, I opened the keepsake book of stories you had written about your life using an online service, a gift from our children and grandchildren. I re-read every story and studied the vintage photos again and again. Then I scrolled back through the photos on my phone, finding images from your birthdays in recent years. There was the one a stranger took of us having dinner at a historic resort. There was another from your birthday during the pandemic when we secluded ourselves in a cabin in Oklahoma. There was another photo of our youngest grandson sitting in your lap, reading your birthday card, as we celebrated with family in California.

All day long, I have felt the emptiness of knowing that the birthday celebrations we once shared are over. Gone. Vanished. At the same time, there is a realization that your years were filled with significance and love. And though it's difficult to accept that you are gone, that is something to celebrate.

———◊———

How will you celebrate the birthday of
your loved one who has died?

My Birthday

Weeks ago, the family asked how they could help celebrate my upcoming birthday. They offered to drive or fly, just to be here with me. Truthfully, I would have preferred to skip my birthday altogether. I didn't feel like celebrating. These months following your death have been brutal, and I am not looking forward to another revolution around the sun without you by my side. Not even a stack of birthday cards or the sweetest sentiments on social media could substitute for your rendition of "Happy Birthday" as you brought me a card and a cup of coffee first thing in the morning. How can I be happy when you are not here?

Now my birthday has arrived, and I have decided to escape the familiar surroundings of home. I've driven over two hundred miles to gather with part of our family. Last night I stayed in a hotel suite with the grandkids and savored their amusing stories along with the digital photos of their summer vacations and camps. For a while, I forgot that I was sad.

Their youthful laughter brought such levity and joy. I only wished you could have been there to share in the moment.

This morning, we all slid onto a church pew for Sunday morning worship at my sister's church. The music, the message, and the hospitality filled my parched soul. But when we stood to sing the final hymn, my throat tightened, and the words would not come. I just bowed my head and let the tears silently fall to the floor. Later, we sat around a long table for my birthday brunch. I looked into the faces of these loved ones: brother, sister, son and daughter-in-law, grandchildren, nephew and niece. They filled me up when I felt depleted, and that is a great gift.

———◊———

What or who fills you up when you feel depleted?

Anniversary of Your Death

The day of your death now marks a square on the calendar. It is a date that divides my life into two parts: before death and after. Now that the anniversary of your death is here, I have a confession: I wish people wouldn't try to cheer me on in celebration of the fact that I have reached this milestone. Yes, I have survived all the firsts of the calendar year following your death—first birthday, first anniversary, first Christmas. Some are almost gleeful when they say, "You've made it through all the firsts!" I know they mean well, but their good intentions frustrate me. I don't want to be congratulated for surviving this past year. I don't want a trophy for clearing the last hurdle on the calendar. To celebrate getting through the all the firsts feels dismissive, as if the pain will somehow miraculously dissipate as I cross the finish line on the anniversary of your death.

Yet I am grateful for those who are aware of your death anniversary. Most people are busy with their own lives and have long forgotten the heartbreaking significance of this day to me. Life continues to be a push-pull of contradicting emotions. One thing I know for certain: Grief is not a matter of getting past all the obstacles of the first year. It's learning to embrace life each day knowing that joy and grief will always be intertwined. Some people say the second year is even more difficult than the first because the initial shock of loss and death is waning. Tomorrow I will still feel pangs of grief throughout the day, but I will keep moving forward.

———◊———

How can you make the most of the rest of the days of your life?